ENCOUNTERS
ON THE ROAD
TO THE CROSS

A Lenten Study for Adults

Encounters on the Road to the Cross

Robert Martin Walker

Abingdon Press
Nashville

ENCOUNTERS ON THE ROAD TO THE CROSS

Copyright © 1998 by Abingdon Press

This book is printed on acid-free, recycled paper.

Library of Congress Cataloging-in-Publication Data

Walker, Robert Martin.
 Encounters on the road to the cross: a Lenten study for adults/
Robert Martin Walker.
  p. cm.
 ISBN 0-687-09539-5 (alk. paper)
  1. Lent—Meditations. 2. Holy Week—Meditations. I. Title.
BV85.W315 1998
242'.34—dc21   97-42417
                                                             CIP

Scripture quotations are from the New Revised Standard Version of the Bible, copyright © 1989 by the Division of Christian Education of the National Council of the Churches of Christ in the USA. Used by permission.

Cover photo: Biblical Archaeology Society © 1981

98 99 00 01 02 03 04 05 06 07 — 10 9 8 7 6 5 4 3

MANUFACTURED IN THE UNITED STATES OF AMERICA

For Evelyn,
whose heart overflows
with self-giving love

CONTENTS

INTRODUCTION

Lent is a time for encountering Jesus. During the forty days of Lent, we follow Jesus from his temptation in the Galilean wilderness to the cross on Golgotha. Although we can follow these events as mildly interested observers, as we would read a history text, there is another way to understand them: as deeply engaged participants.

When we make the movement from observer to participant, we become part of the journey to the cross. Observers stand by the roadside and watch Jesus struggle under the weight of the cross. Participants take up their own crosses and follow. Observers watch the crucified Lord from a distance. Participants hang on their own crosses next to the Lord.

One of the ways we can become participants in the Lenten drama is through the men and women who encountered Jesus on the road to the cross. This requires that we use our God-given imagination. With imagination, we become the rich man hearing the challenge to give all his possessions to the poor and follow Jesus. With an imaginative leap, we are the woman at the well, conversing with Jesus about living water.

Imagination is at the heart of compassion, which literally means "to suffer with." If we can imagine what it is like to be naked, poor, unemployed, or ill, then we can understand the plight of those who suffer these difficulties.

Imagination also has a great deal to do with faith. The author of Hebrews has given us this definition of faith: "the assurance of things hoped for, the conviction of things not seen" (11:1). What a powerful suggestion that imagination is the gateway to faith.

My hope for this study is that your imagination will be engaged through these seven characters whose lives intersected Jesus' ministry. The characters tell of their encounters with Jesus from their own points of view, enabling us to see and experience new possibilities in the biblical text. The mixture of imagination and interpretation varies from character to character. Where the Bible is silent, imagination fills the spaces. Where the Bible speaks, I have attempted to be faithful to the scriptural text, sometimes following it word for word.

As we stand in these characters' shoes (or sandals), seeing Jesus through their eyes, we will become more deeply engaged in the journey to the cross. Through their encounters with Jesus, may you come to better know Jesus and understand what it means for you to encounter him in your own life and time.

Robert Martin Walker

First Week in Lent

THE RICH YOUNG MAN

Read Mark 10:17-22

Twenty years have passed since I knelt at the feet of Jesus. I was young then, full of dreams and plans. My future was wide open, as promising and fertile as the fields of Canaan. Yet I was not content. Even though I had everything a young man could desire, I was searching.

For what? I didn't know then and still am not sure. I suspected there must be something more to life than the pleasures and enjoyments my wealth provided. My friends assured me that there was nothing money couldn't buy. But why did I feel dissatisfied with my life?

My restlessness was ironic. All that I desired, I had acquired. I was rich beyond imagining. After my father died, I had inherited his farm and multiplied it into a great fortune. Because of my shrewdness and toil, I no longer had to worry about money. I could live in luxury with servants scurrying to fulfill my every request.

Strangely, I found that as soon as one desire was fulfilled, another arose to take its place. I was living from desire to desire, but contentment eluded me.

It was then that emptiness descended upon me like fog on the Kidron Valley at daybreak. Since I didn't have to do anything, there was no necessity to my life, no sense of purpose or direction. Even running a successful farm became unsatisfying. I was bored with life, not knowing which way to turn.

Even the religion of my father offered no relief. A pious and devout man, he had lived strictly by the Torah. The life of daily prayers and reading the Scriptures had seemed to be enough for him. Despite having achieved only a fraction of my wealth, he had been content with his life.

As a boy, I had memorized the Torah in synagogue school. I had tried to live by the spirit of Torah as well as its letter. As a young man, I became as devout as a rabbi. Daily, I went to pray in the synagogue. I gave a double tithe of alms, which gained the attention of the priests. I tried to achieve contentment through devotion.

Why it wasn't enough for me to follow the way of Torah, I don't know. All I know is that I was seeking something, anything that would soothe my aching spirit.

One day, at my lowest point, I heard that a great rabbi called Jesus was coming to town. He had a reputation as an amazing teacher. Reportedly, the crowds who heard him were astonished by his teachings. I joined the large crowd who had gathered on the road to walk with Jesus and listen to him speak.

I was too far back in the crowd to hear his words at first. I pushed my way to the front in time to see several children surrounding Jesus. His hands were resting on the head of a little girl and boy as he said, "I tell you the truth: Whoever does not receive the kingdom of God like a little child will never enter it."

That was it! Jesus had named what I was searching for: the kingdom of God. He started walking down the Jerusalem road. On a wild impulse, I broke free from the crowd and bowed down at Jesus' feet.

Out of emptiness and need I blurted out, "Good teacher, what must I do to have eternal life?" He recited the commandments from the Torah that I knew so well. With deep sincerity, I answered that I had been following the Torah from my youth.

Was it pity or compassion I read in Jesus' eyes? I felt that he cared deeply about me, a stranger asking a desperate question. He seemed to know why I had asked. It was as if he was looking deep into my soul and saw the void there.

What he said to me I will never forget: "You lack one thing; go, sell what you own, and give the money to the poor, and you will have treasure in heaven; then come, follow me."

I was stunned. Jesus' words pierced me like a centurion's sword. Was he blind to the fine clothing and expensive rings I wore? Did he not know the impossibility of what he was asking of me?

My wealth was my armor, my protection against the hardships and sufferings of life. Money meant security. Without it, I would be naked and vulnerable. I couldn't bring myself to imagine giving away my hard-earned fortune to the undeserving poor! My prosperity was a sign of God's favor. Didn't he realize my success resulted from my faithfulness to God's will?

My decision was made in an instant. I knew that I couldn't leave my great fortune behind and follow Jesus into an unknown future. Only a fool would be so reckless. How could treasures in heaven surpass earthly riches?

Yet there was a part of me that wanted to follow Jesus, even on such extreme terms. My emptiness cried out, but my fears drowned out the inner voice that begged me to do what he had asked. I was terrified of taking this leap into the unknown. To follow Jesus would mean being at the mercy of uncertainty—wandering from town to town, dependent upon others for food and lodging. Who would willingly live this way?

I had too much to give up. I wanted to follow, but not under such radical conditions. I wanted to follow Jesus *and* keep my wealth. But this option was not offered. To follow Jesus meant leaving every-thing behind. I walked away in sorrowful silence, never to see him again.

After a few minutes, my sorrow turned into anger, and anger transformed itself into indignation. "How dare he ask such an impossible thing!" I shouted aloud to myself. "He can't even imagine the difficulty of what he is asking of me. Who is he to tell me that I lack something?" I was seething, outraged that he demanded such a soul-wrenching choice. Rage drove out the sorrow—for a time.

Three months after my encounter with Jesus, I learned that he had been crucified like a common criminal. His death was a terrible tragedy that robbed the world of a great rabbi. Instead of feeling sadness at this news, I felt relieved! Jesus' crucifixion confirmed that I had indeed made the right choice. I could have ended up on a cross too, had I been so foolish to give away my wealth and travel with him on the road to Jerusalem.

As I said, that happened twenty years ago. Recently, I have started wondering how different my life might have been if I had followed Jesus. What roads would I have traveled? What strange twists and turns would my life have taken? Would I have found what I was seeking? I still haven't discovered the cure for the disease of unhap-piness. Oh, I've become accustomed to it and have learned to live with it. I have my distractions: running my business, dining with friends, traveling. But I occasionally wonder whether giving up my wealth and following Jesus would have satisfied me.

Regardless, I missed my chance. Having once refused, I thought it was too late for me to follow—until a few days ago. A stranger calling himself a Christian told me that after Jesus was crucified he was raised to new life by God. He also said something that rekindled my yearning for something more. "All who believe in him will be raised to a new life too," he said.

Wistfully, I told him the story of walking away from Jesus so many years ago. Amazingly, this stranger wasn't shocked at my rejection.

He said that many had rejected Jesus when he was alive, including himself. He assured me that it is never too late to follow Jesus and live.

Perhaps this time, I will follow.

PRAYER

Dear Lord, you call me to follow you without counting the cost. I confess that I have calculated the price of loyalty to you. Forgive my weakness of will and give me the strength to walk in the way that leads to abundant life. In Jesus' name I pray. Amen.

STUDY/DISCUSSION QUESTIONS

1. What was the source of the rich young man's discontentment? Why do you think his youth and wealth were not enough to bring him lasting happiness? When have *you* experienced the emptiness of discontentment? What led to this experience?
2. What issues were involved in the young man's struggle over whether to follow Jesus? What seemed to be the key factor in his decision not to follow Jesus? In what ways do you identify with his decision? When have you faced a similar choice?
3. Why wasn't the young man able to give up his wealth and follow Jesus? Was his anger over being asked to give up everything he owned justified? How would you have felt if confronted with such a decision? What are you being asked to give up in order to follow Jesus' way of discipleship?
4. Read Mark 10:23-27, the passage that follows the story of the rich young man. How is wealth/affluence a barrier to following Jesus? What should be our attitude toward wealth and its proper place in life?

DEEPENING YOUR LENTEN JOURNEY: SELF-EXAMINATION

- The practice of giving up something for Lent is a well-established tradition. As a variation on this tradition, consider "taking on" a new Lenten discipline, such as having a daily time of prayer, doing a special act of service, or reading a book to enrich your faith.
- John Wesley's advice on money was to earn all you can, save all you can, and give all you can. Take a few minutes to reflect on

how you are using your money. In what ways are you spending money responsibly? What portion of your wealth are you giving to help those in need? What good are you accomplishing with your wealth?

• Make a list of "Ways I Can Be a More Faithful Disciple of Christ." Circle one or two items on the list that you are willing to work on now. Save the list to remind yourself of that commitment.

THE WOMAN CAUGHT IN ADULTERY

Read John 7:53–8:11

I had just embraced my lover when two men burst through the door, with my husband following. The strangers jerked me out of bed and forced me to stand before them in shame. My lover, Benjamin, was allowed to dress and leave without a word said to him.

"Aha!" said one of the two bearded men, "You have been caught, and now you must pay the price!" He sounded almost gleeful. He and the other man wore the robes of Pharisees.

My husband, Levi, stood before me and spat in my face. "Adulteress!" he said. Then he hurled my robe at me and said, "Put this on. We're going to the temple." The expression on his face said, "Vengeance will be sweet."

After I dressed, the bearded men stood on each side of me and grasped my arms roughly. They escorted me through the streets of Jerusalem like Roman soldiers taking a prisoner to execution. I felt the burning of eyes on my back as my neighbors came out of their houses to see the spectacle. It was as if everyone knew what I had done. Several followed in my sin-parade, picking up stones by the roadside.

During the forced march to the temple, the enormity of my sin began to weigh upon me, and tears streamed down my cheeks. My entire body shook like a reed in the wind. I was wrong to have loved a man other than my husband. For months I had justified my adultery by thinking about Levi's harsh treatment of me. Our arranged marriage was without love, without kindness, without intimacy. I was a woman with normal desires, which Levi ignored. We no longer shared the same bed. We spoke only when necessary, and then about trivial matters. Our marriage was a sham. According to the law, I could not divorce Levi; only a man could divorce his wife.

I wasn't excusing my sin, but explaining it to myself. No one would understand my pain, anyway. In a matter of minutes, my inner ache would be replaced by physical pain. And then it would be over. I was being taken to the temple to be stoned to death. The Torah was clear about the penalty for a woman caught in adultery. At least Benjamin would live.

All eyes were upon me as we ascended the temple steps. Those in our train cried, "Adulteress!" and "Stone her!" I looked down as I walked, not wanting to meet the eyes of my accusers. To my surprise, I was not led into the chambers of the council of seventy-one, where trials were held. Rather, I was led to a man who was sitting in a corner of the temple court, speaking to a crowd. The crowd parted as I was hauled before him. Every conversation in the temple stopped.

The Pharisee who tightly held my right arm let go and pushed me forward so that I was standing alone before the crowd. I felt the weight of humiliation even more intensely.

He addressed the man who was sitting: "Rabbi, this woman was caught in the very act of adultery!" Hisses came from the crowd. "The law of Moses commands us to stone her. What do you say?"

The rabbi didn't even look up at my accuser; instead, he bent down and began writing in the dirt with a finger. I caught a glimpse of disgust on his face. Suddenly, I realized why I was brought here. My husband had conspired with these Pharisees to entrap me! They must have been waiting outside the door, listening for the sounds of passion. Levi knew that I had been seeing another man, but didn't care as long as we were discreet. He could have divorced me at any time. Instead, he set a trap. But *why?*

The Pharisees shocked me out of my reverie by hurling questions at the sitting rabbi. They kept asking him, "What do you say? What do you say?" They were like jackals circling their prey, using words instead of snarls. Finally, the man stopped writing in the dirt and looked at them, his back rigid with anger. I waited to hear him join the Pharisees in condemning me. How else could he answer?

He said, "Let anyone among you who is without sin be the first to throw a stone at her."

This wasn't the expected answer. The crowd stood as silent as the stones they held. I closed my eyes and waited for the first blow to fall. Then I heard sounds of feet shuffling on the temple floor. I stole a sideways glance. One by one, the crowd was leaving!

Within minutes, I was standing alone before the rabbi. Again, he wrote in the dirt. I began to tremble, not knowing what to expect from this man who could scatter the powerful with a single sentence. I stood motionless, as though my feet had grown roots. I could barely breathe.

Again the rabbi straightened his back and looked at me. His eyes were kind and gentle, but his mouth was firmly set. Would I receive the mercy of his eyes, or the judgment of his mouth?

He said, "Woman, is there no one left to condemn you?"

I said quietly, "No one, Lord."

He paused and I waited to hear my fate. Anyone who spoke with such authority could condemn me with a single word.

Finally, he said, "Neither do I condemn you. Go your way and do not sin again."

My knees buckled. I kept hearing those words, "Neither do I condemn you," over and over in my mind. I had entered the temple as a condemned sinner; I walked out a forgiven sinner.

I walked through the temple court with my back straight. Those who were hoping to stone me cast scornful looks, but no stones. Such was the authority of the rabbi who freed me.

It has taken time to grasp the enormity of that day. Because of the mercy of the rabbi, Jesus (I have since learned his name), I have a second chance at life. My sin was inexcusable, but it was forgiven. For the first few days after my meeting with Jesus, I bathed in the glory of my pardon. It was as if I had died and was alive again. Then, Jesus' final words began to work on my conscience: "Go and do not sin again."

I began to live my second life differently. First, I forgave Levi for setting a trap for me. Perhaps he was used by the Pharisees as I was. Then, I asked Levi to forgive my adultery. He said nothing, but he didn't divorce me. I have tried to be a loving wife, difficult as it is. Levi and I have hurt each other much. With love and time, I pray our hearts will heal.

And what became of Jesus? I hear that the Pharisees were so enraged by his words that they wanted to arrest him. They had used me as bait, hoping to snare a larger prize, but Jesus had not fallen into their trap. Levi tells me they are seeking other ways to trick him into violating the law. Strangely, Levi has said nothing bad about Jesus. He even admitted that Jesus is a "good man." I, however, think he is much more.

PRAYER

Dear Lord of forgiveness, I confess that I have sinned by what I have done and what I haven't done. Like the woman caught in adultery, I stand before you waiting for your verdict. Give me the power to accept your forgiveness and to forgive those who have wronged me. In Jesus' name I pray. Amen.

STUDY/DISCUSSION QUESTIONS

1. The story of the woman caught in adultery is not included in the oldest manuscripts of the Gospels. However, most Bibles include

it with a footnote (see the footnote in the NRSV). Does this story seem authentic to you? Why or why not? How is the Jesus of this story consistent with the Jesus we see in the Gospels?

2. Do you believe that the woman was "set up" by the Pharisees? Why or why not? How did the Pharisees use her to try to entrap Jesus? When have you felt used by others? How did you react?

3. If the woman was entrapped, does it excuse her adultery? Is her self-justification believable? Why or why not? How do we justify/rationalize our sins? What breaks down our rationalizations of sin?

4. How would you have felt after hearing Jesus' words of forgiveness? What do you think happened to the woman after this encounter with Jesus? Do you think she was changed by this encounter? In what ways?

DEEPENING YOUR LENTEN JOURNEY: FORGIVENESS

- Make a list of your sins for the past week. This list could include both wrongs committed and goods omitted. You also might want to add to your list ways you have fallen short of the person you aspire to be. After completing this list, read each sin aloud and say, "In the name of Christ, I am forgiven."

- Take a few moments to reflect on a person whom you find difficult to forgive. This person may have hurt or used you in some painful way. This person may not have asked for your forgiveness. After naming this person, say aloud, "I forgive you." It may take time before the inner pain this person has caused will go away. But by saying "I forgive you," you will begin the healing process.

- Not only did Jesus forgive the woman caught in adultery, but he also told her, "From now on do not sin again" (John 8:11). Traditionally, Lent is a time of repentance. What do you need to repent of? Focus on one aspect of yourself that you need to change. Allow God's forgiveness to work its power to enable you to change this permanently and to "not sin again."

Third Week in Lent

THE WOMAN AT THE WELL

Read John 4:4-42

Yesterday, when news spread that a great rabbi called Jesus was coming to Samaria, my heart soared. In the market, I had overheard the excited gossip of the "respectable" women who chattered about the amazing signs Jesus was said to perform (even changing water into wine!). I yearned to see him, but at the same time, I was afraid.

Part of my apprehension was because I am a Samaritan. Jews and Samaritans hate each other. Our dispute with the Jews goes back many centuries, to the time of the Exile. We courageously remained in Judah when the Jews were taken east to Babylonia. Because we intermarried with people who migrated there, the Jews call us half-breeds. And because we believe that our ancestor, Moses, received the sacred tablets of law on Mount Gerizim, we are called heretics. We built our temple on Mount Gerizim, and the Jews built theirs in Jerusalem (an issue we have heatedly argued about for centuries). Jews and Samaritans have nothing to do with each other. A Jew will not look upon a Samaritan, let alone speak to one.

Perhaps this is why I was so eager to meet Jesus, a great Jewish rabbi who risked his own people's scorn by traveling to Samaria. "He must have a good reason for coming here," I assured myself.

The morning he was to arrive, I awoke early and did my chores. As usual, I went to the well to draw water at first light (to avoid the other women). Since Jesus was coming from Judea, about twenty miles south, he wouldn't be arriving until midday. I passed the morning in the south end of the fields where I could see the road to Jacob's well. My hands were gleaning grain, but my mind was occupied with Jesus.

When I saw a band of a dozen men approaching the well, I ran home for my water jar. I was terrified of being confronted by so many Jewish men, but if I was to meet Jesus, there was no other choice.

When I arrived at the well, one man was sitting alone in the shade of an olive tree. My heart was pounding as I realized that he was probably Jesus. He startled me by asking for a drink of water. I hid my shaking hands behind my back as I reminded him of the social customs he was ignoring by speaking to me.

The Woman at the Well 21

"How is it that you, a Jew, ask a drink of me, a woman of Samaria?"

Not only did Jews refuse to speak to Samaritans; a rabbi would never address a strange woman without first being introduced.

Jesus made an unusual remark. He said that if I knew who he was, I would have asked *him* for a drink of "living water." I was intimidated by this challenge because I didn't know what "living water" was. Could he be speaking of the sweet, cold water that bubbles up from a spring? So I asked, "Where do you get this living water?"

When he was silent, I risked a challenge of my own. "Are you greater than our father, Jacob, who gave us this well?"

Jesus ignored the question and spoke more about living water. He explained that those who drink it would never again be thirsty, and that those who possessed it would have eternal life. I was utterly bewildered by these words. I didn't understand what he meant, but I knew I wanted to taste this living water. So I asked him for a drink (just as he said I would).

After I had fulfilled his prediction, an incredible thought started to take shape in my mind: Perhaps Jesus was more than a rabbi. Was he a prophet?

While musing on this, the conversation took a threatening turn. Jesus asked me to tell my husband to come there. My heart raced, and my hands grew damp. Could this man I had never met know my secret? Did he know *everything* about me?

I side-stepped the truth. "I have no husband," I said.

Jesus then showed that he truly was a prophet. He told me that I had answered correctly, because I had had *five* husbands, and the man who was now sharing my bed wasn't my husband. I was stunned. He *did* know my past, a past of which I was deeply ashamed. I felt naked—exposed.

If Jesus knew my past, did he also know about the cruel teasing, the painful rejections, and the humiliating mockery I had to endure daily? Did he hear the whispers of women when I walked into the village market? Did he see how the men leered at me, as if I would gladly welcome any of them to my bed? Did he know that some men would brush up against me and purposely touch me? Did he realize that men had offered me money to share their beds, as if I were a cheap prostitute?

After my plunge into self-pity, another, even wilder, thought arose: Could Jesus be the prophet-Messiah hoped for by my people?

I decided to test him. If he were the Messiah, he could decide who was right about an issue of fierce dispute between Jews and Samaritans: Where ought God to be worshiped? Jerusalem or Mount Gerizim?

Jesus' answer astounded me. He spoke of a coming day when God would not be worshiped in a holy place, but in "spirit and in truth." What a revolutionary idea! Did Jesus realize what he was saying? He could be killed for voicing such radical notions. We—and the Jews—believed that the place where God was worshiped was of the utmost importance. If location was not crucial, it meant we were free to worship God *anywhere*! This impossible idea overwhelmed me.

From deep within myself, I summoned the courage to discover who Jesus really was. I offered him the opportunity to reveal himself by saying, "When the Messiah comes, he will show us all things."

Jesus replied, "I who speak to you am he."

I stood there motionless, my wide eyes transfixed on him.

Suddenly, his disciples returned and were clearly irritated that Jesus was speaking to me. They asked, accusingly, "Why are you talking to her?"

Without waiting to hear Jesus' answer, I fled! I left so quickly, I forgot my water jar. Running into the village, I told anyone who would listen about my conversation with Jesus. When they were skeptical, I challenged, "Come and see a man who told me all that I ever did. He could be the Messiah!"

As I retold my story to each person, I began to realize something about the living water of which Jesus spoke. A sense of excitement welled up within me. An inner change was taking place. As my belief that Jesus was the Messiah grew, it was as if a spring of new life was bubbling inside of me! Had Jesus already given me living water?

From that day on, I led a new life, putting my past behind me. I had lived for myself only; now, I would live for Him. Jesus and his gift of living water changed everything. He broke the dam of guilt that held my failures and sins within me. After meeting Jesus, the guilt flowed out, leaving me cleansed and free.

The living water that Jesus offers is the most precious gift of all. To drink of it is to drink deeply of Jesus' spirit of love and truth. Once your thirst for new life has been satisfied, you will be content, no longer thirsting for pleasure, power, or wealth—no longer burdened by the crushing weight of guilt and self-condemnation. Living water, the Spirit of Jesus, means peace with God.

One more thing. You can't contain the excitement of living water. The joy overflows! You want to share this precious gift with everyone you meet. You *must* invite them to come and see for themselves the Christ who gives the gift of living water.

PRAYER

Lord of Life, lead me to the well of living water so that I may drink deeply. Let the joy of your Spirit flow within me like a rushing brook. May your love overflow so that the precious gift of new life is shared through me. In Jesus' name I pray. Amen.

STUDY/DISCUSSION QUESTIONS

1. What is the "living water" Jesus offered the woman: Jesus' spirit, Jesus' teachings, new life, or all three? When have you been aware of your thirst for living water? How has this thirst been satisfied? What enabled the woman at the well to receive the gift of living water? What allows you to receive this gift?
2. Reflect on the fact that Jesus was breaking social, cultural, and religious boundaries when he spoke to the Samaritan woman. Why do you think Jesus traveled through Samaria? What did he accomplish in his conversation with the woman at the well? When has your faith caused you to cross social, cultural, or religious boundaries?
3. How did Jesus reveal the "truth" about the woman's life? When has an encounter with Jesus exposed the truth about your life? What was your reaction to hearing the truth about yourself?
4. Think about how much our worship is related to a particular place: a church, a chapel, or a retreat center. What physical setting is most worshipful for you? What does it mean to worship God "in spirit and in truth"?

DEEPENING YOUR LENTEN JOURNEY:
NEW LIFE

- When the Samaritan woman learned that Jesus is the Christ, she ran into her village and shared the good news with everyone. Reflect on ways you can share your faith with others. Often, conversations such as the one that took place between Jesus and the woman are vehicles for speaking about what matters deeply to you.
- One practical way of sharing a gift of life with others is to donate blood. Contact your local Red Cross to learn the date of the next blood drive and to see whether you qualify. Another way of

sharing life is giving the gift of food through a church or local food pantry.

- Break down cultural barriers by inviting to dinner a family from a culture different from your own. Use the table conversation as an opportunity to learn about a new culture. This kind of meal can promote mutual understanding.

The Mother of James and John

Read Matthew 4:21-22; 20:20-28; 27:55-56

I was confused when my husband, Zebedee, burst into the kitchen and said, "They're gone."

"Who's gone?" I asked.

He said, "Our boys. They left with a stranger named Jesus." I could see where tears had streaked Zebedee's cheeks.

I sat down on the floor. "How? Why?"

Zebedee took a deep breath and told me the story. The three of them were in the boat, not far from shore, mending their nets after a night's fishing on the Sea of Galilee. There was the usual relaxed banter that followed a good catch. Then this stranger on the shore walked close to them, with Simon and Andrew following. He looked intently at James and John, who seemed captivated by him. The stranger called out, "Follow me!" Without a second thought, our boys left their father alone in the boat and waded to shore. Within minutes, they had faded into the distance.

"They didn't even say good-bye," Zebedee lamented. "I asked Simon and Andrew's father who the stranger was and what had happened. The only word he said was 'Jesus.' "

"All the stranger said was 'follow me'?" I cried.

"Yes. That was it," Zebedee said, his voice laced with grief and disbelief. We sat on the kitchen floor, weeping and holding each other, but we were not comforted.

So it was that my boys became followers of the rabbi Jesus. I wasn't sure who took their leaving harder, me or Zebedee, until he died a few months later. I think he died of a broken heart. He and the boys were so close; they did everything together. I was devastated by this triple loss.

James and John came home to visit soon after their father's death. Somehow, my message had reached them. It was the first time I had seen them since they left. My, how they had changed. They had always been loud and filled with energy. Now, they were quieter, more reflective. James, the older of the two, reassured me that they still loved me and were sorry not to have been able to say good-bye to their father. "But we have been on an important mission," he said.

Then they told me the most amazing things about Jesus, whom they called "the Lord." They said that he was a teacher sent from God. They took turns retelling his wise parables. They regaled me with how Jesus had healed the sick, even raising the dead to life! They claimed that Jesus was the long-awaited Messiah. I wasn't sure what to believe about all of this.

But I was most intrigued when they spoke about the kingdom that Jesus was planning to establish. This kingdom was to be God's reign on earth, with Jesus as the sovereign. It would be a kingdom more glorious than the Roman Empire, and Jesus would be more powerful than the Emperor. My boys' faces glowed as they spoke of it.

Until then, I thought James and John had been on a fool's errand. However, I began to see an interesting possibility. If Jesus were to become king, then my boys could be seconds-in-command. I wondered if they were clever enough to recognize their good fortune.

"Do you realize what Jesus' coming into power could mean for you?" I asked. "You could rule with him!"

I saw by the spark in their eyes that they had considered this possibility and were pleased by it. I explained that it would be better if someone other than themselves would approach Jesus on their behalf. If they appeared greedy, they might hurt their chances of sharing Lord Jesus' power. I offered to plead their case, and they quickly agreed.

On the two-day journey to catch up with Jesus and his other followers, I savored the opportunity that was about to unfold for James and John. Being a fisherman is fine; it puts food on the table and a roof over your head. But here was a chance for my sons to be something more. Perhaps they could achieve a measure of greatness! And, of course, the mother of the king's lieutenants would be highly regarded.

When we arrived at Jericho, the place where Jesus was teaching, I walked right up to him with my boys in tow. Wasting no time, I knelt down and asked if I might be granted a favor.

"What is it that you want?" Jesus asked quietly.

"My Lord, I would ask you to declare that my two sons will sit on each side of you in your kingdom."

Jesus said, "You have no idea what you are asking." Then he addressed James and John: "Are you able to drink the cup I am about to drink?"

"We are able, Lord," they said, almost in unison.

Jesus' voice took on a serious quality. "You will drink my cup. But to sit on my right and left is my Father's decision."

I could hear angry grumbles behind me. There was obviously

some envy on the part of the other ten disciples of Jesus. I had little sympathy for them; if they wanted to rule with Jesus, they should have thought to ask him. I was pleased that my boys were the first to stake their claim to power.

James and John defended my actions, and an argument erupted over who should sit at Jesus' right hand. Simon seemed especially upset. I had learned from James and John that he was their main rival for second-in-command.

Jesus' voice rose over the quarrel. He sounded angrier than any of the others. "Do you think my kingdom is like that of the Gentiles, where the rulers are tyrants? No! Whoever wants to be greatest among you must be the slave of the rest. For I came not to be served but to serve, and to give my life for many."

We were all stunned into silence. I was bewildered about the meaning of Jesus' words. The greatest will be a *slave*? What kind of nonsense was this? And what did he mean by saying that he was giving his life for others? I walked away feeling disappointed for my sons and puzzled about what kind of king would say the things Jesus had said.

As I was leaving, I saw a group of women who were near my age standing a short distance away. I stopped to chat, trying to forget my confusion. When I mentioned Jesus, they began to tell me what they had witnessed. They provided many more details than my sons. I was amazed at their stories and impressed by their faith that Jesus was God's very son. The long and short of that meeting was that I became a follower of Jesus! Along with Mary, the Lord's mother, Mary Magdalene, and Mary, the mother of James and Joseph, I helped support the mission of Jesus and his disciples. We bought food, cooked, and did whatever chores were needed. I guess we became like the "slaves" Jesus spoke of the first time I met him.

That's how I ended up watching the Lord die. We, the women, stood at a distance from the cross, feeling helpless to stop the tragedy. As I saw him breathe his last, I finally understood what he had said to me that day about his kingdom. He was the King of love. And with my own eyes, I watched the greatest act of love I had ever seen.

PRAYER

Dear Lord of love, forgive my selfish ambition to be first in your kingdom. Teach me the way of servanthood and self-giving love. Remold me so that I am able to follow you with my heart, soul, mind, and strength. In Jesus' name I pray. Amen.

Study/Discussion Questions

1. What kind of person was the mother of James and John before meeting Jesus? At what points can you identify with her story? What might have motivated her to ask her "favor" of Jesus? Why do you think she didn't understand Jesus' answer to her?
2. Read Mark 9:33-37. Does it surprise you that the disciples argued among themselves? Why or why not? What character traits do you see in James and John? How does Jesus respond to the disciples' misunderstanding of his kingdom?
3. What kind of "kingdom" did Jesus establish? What character traits and attitudes should the "subjects" of this kingdom possess? What does it mean for you to live as part of Jesus' kingdom? In what ways do you put the concept of servanthood into action?
4. Matthew 27:55-56 lists several women who supported Jesus' ministry and witnessed his crucifixion. How do you imagine that these women supported Jesus' mission? What other roles did women play in Jesus' ministry? What roles do women fill in the church today?

Deepening Your Lenten Journey:
Servanthood

- This week, look for ways to serve others. Your service might take the form of showing kindness to a family member, spending time with someone who is lonely, making a phone call to a neglected friend, or volunteering to do a needed job in the church. The key is to do something that has no direct benefit to you. However, if you feel a sense of satisfaction at having served, that's only natural.
- Carefully read and reflect on each verse of the hymn "Are Ye Able." Imagine that Jesus is asking you each of the questions that form the verses of this hymn. How will you answer?
- One way to enact servanthood is to literally serve food to others. Volunteer time at a local soup kitchen or food bank. As you offer food to others, realize that you are giving a gift of life.
- Reflect on the following statement: "God made the world in such a way that those who lay down their life for others receive genuine life." What ways are you "laying down" your life for others? How do you receive life by such acts of self-giving love?

CAIAPHAS THE HIGH PRIEST

Read Matthew 26:57-68; 27:3-31, 62-66; 28:11-15

For months I have agonized over the Jesus Problem. This carpenter's son from Galilee torments me, even in my dreams. Some nights I wake in a panic and worry until dawn over what to do about the threat he poses.

Jesus of Nazareth has been gaining daily in popularity and power. Thousands of ignorant souls have been flocking out into the countryside like stupid sheep to hear him teach and see him "heal." These fools have been taken in by his so-called miracles. Hah!

When reports about Jesus first reached me, I wasn't concerned. He seemed like another small-time traveling rabbi with a handful of deluded followers. In my eighteen years as high priest, I have had the displeasure of dealing with a dozen of these charlatans. They fade away once my lawyers attack them publicly.

But Jesus is different. Three times I sent my most devious legal experts to entrap him. Each time, he turned their words back upon them. These so-called experts were the ones slinking away in humiliation. Imbeciles!

Two months ago I heard that some of Jesus' followers were calling him "Messiah"! My heart was chilled. I knew that he couldn't possibly be the Messiah. He was nothing like the triumphant king described by the prophets. Yet, if his followers believed this lie, they could stir up trouble. The ludicrous idea that Jesus was the Messiah coupled with his growing popularity made him an increasingly dangerous adversary.

Further, my spies reported that he had condemned some of my fellow Sanhedrin members for hypocrisy. One spy said that Jesus had threatened to tear down the temple! To threaten God's temple is blasphemy.

When I heard that he was coming to Jerusalem, I knew something had to be done about the Jesus Problem before it got out of control. I presented my case to the Sanhedrin and convinced them that Jesus must be arrested for blasphemy. I wanted it done quietly, and without the threat of a riot.

Day after day my guards stalked Jesus and his followers, but we couldn't get close enough to arrest him because of the surrounding crowds.

Finally, just before Jesus entered the gates of the Holy City, an opportunity to put an end to the Jesus Problem presented itself. Late one night, Judas, son of Iscariot, one of Jesus' disciples, came to me with a proposition. I was stunned, and delighted, that one of Jesus' own followers would deliver him into our hands, and for so little money. Thirty pieces of silver was all that Judas demanded for his act of treachery. I wondered why he would do this for so little money, but I didn't satisfy my curiosity, for fear of his demanding more. I couldn't believe my good fortune! Ending the Jesus Problem was going to be easier than I had imagined.

My hopes, however, quickly turned into fears. We didn't hear from Judas for several days, and my spies lost track of Jesus. Then, on the first day of the week of the Feast of Unleavened Bread, I heard loud cheers coming from outside the temple gates. "Hosanna!" the crowds were yelling. I asked one of my servants to determine the source of the commotion. He returned and reported that Jesus had ridden into the city like an ancient king! He was riding on a donkey, the correct mount for a triumphant king. I tore my clothes with rage! I had been tricked by Judas! The betrayer had betrayed me!

My worst nightmare had come true: Jesus had entered Jerusalem to take away my power!

To my astonishment, Jesus went into hiding again. He didn't seize his opportunity to become a king! He squandered his moment of glory! Was this some clever strategy, or was it stupidity?

I was unable to sleep for fear that Jesus would come out of hiding and elude my trap. I had every guard and spy searching the city for even a rumor of Jesus' hideaway. He could not be found.

Last night, my ill luck changed. Judas reappeared. I was lying in bed, staring at the ceiling, when one of my soldiers brought the good news. Judas was shaking as he told me to have my soldiers come at midnight to a garden on the Mount of Olives called Gethsemane. I would find Jesus there, he said.

"How will my guards know which one Jesus is in the darkness?" I asked.

"Arrest them all. One of them can identify him," Judas said.

Over Judas' protests, I insisted that he go with my guards to point out Jesus. He finally relented when I threatened to arrest *him* instead. He said that he would go up to Jesus and kiss him. What wonderful irony, I thought: to betray with a *kiss*.

To prepare for Jesus' arrival, I ordered my guards to summon the Sanhedrin, even though the hour was late. I wasn't taking any chances that Jesus would be tried publicly. I dispatched two guards to rouse several false witnesses to testify against Jesus.

Sometime after midnight, I heard the loud trampling of soldiers' boots in the temple courtyard. My heart pounded with excitement. Jesus was *mine*!

When they hauled him into the council room, I was astonished at my adversary's appearance. Jesus looked seedy and common, with deep furrows of exhaustion under his eyes. He had the haunted look of one who had been betrayed. Rather than appearing as a triumphant king, he was a defeated peasant.

I announced the trial's beginning and read the charge of "blasphemy." We had witness after witness testify against Jesus. To my horror, none of their testimonies agreed. The idiots who bribed them hadn't bothered to rehearse their testimonies! Our law required two witnesses to agree in order to convict a man.

To my relief, the final two witnesses testified that Jesus had said that he would "destroy the temple and rebuild it in three days." This provided the slim opening I needed. I leaped to my feet and demanded that Jesus answer these charges of blasphemy. Jesus had declared himself an enemy of the temple by threatening to destroy it, I shouted.

Strangely, Jesus was silent. He stood motionless, like a statue, with eyes downcast. The fool offered no defense! I taunted him, hoping to trick him into incriminating himself. The testimony of the witnesses was enough to convict Jesus, but it wasn't enough to merit a death sentence.

Then I said, "I put you under oath before the living God: Tell us if you are the Messiah, the Son of God."

To my utter disbelief, Jesus said exactly what I hoped he would. He said quietly, "You have said so."

To underscore this blasphemy, I tore my clothes and screamed, "He has blasphemed! Why do we need witnesses? We all heard it!" I went for the kill: "What is your verdict?"

The Sanhedrin, even those who might have been lenient toward Jesus, yelled angrily, "He deserves death!" With the sentence pronounced, the trial was over. Several members of the council leaped out of their seats and spat on Jesus. Others struck him. A few hurled mocks and insults at him: "Prophesy to us, Messiah! Who hit you?" I couldn't have been more pleased.

There was just one final obstacle to overcome: carrying out the death sentence. The Romans had taken away our power to execute for religious crimes. Although the sentence for blasphemy was death by stoning, the Roman governors were reluctant to put blasphemers to death. Of course, they had no problem crucifying men and women for crimes against Rome.

Reluctantly, I sent Jesus to Governor Pilate with a sealed account of the trial and the sentence pronounced by the Sanhedrin.

Shortly after the trial ended, Judas appeared. With labored steps he dragged himself before me. He was hunched over, clutching his stomach and shaking as though he had a fever.

He wailed, "I have sinned by betraying innocent blood!"

Having no sympathy for traitors, I said, "That's *your* problem. Your Messiah is going to *die!*"

Judas hurled the silver pieces at my feet and fled. That same day, one of my soldiers reported that Judas had hanged himself. Instead of putting the blood money back into the treasury, we bought a potter's field to bury foreigners and other scum like Judas.

Just after Judas left, one of my servants burst into the council room saying that Pilate was going to release a prisoner. In horror, I realized he might have *Jesus* in mind.

Each year during Passover, Pilate would free one prisoner to show what a generous ruler he was. He knew how deeply Roman rule was resented by the people. Like tossing a hungry dog a table scrap, he set one prisoner free. The crowds would choose who would be released by shouting out the name.

I immediately called the chief priests together. We devised a plan to make certain Jesus wasn't released.

It was only an hour before Pilate was to address the people of Jerusalem. I summoned the Sanhedrin once again and explained our dire situation and the plan for stopping Pilate. We infiltrated the crowd gathered in front of the governor's palace like bees in a hive. We spread the word that Jesus was a blasphemer and that he had threatened to destroy the temple. We spread silver pieces liberally among the crowd to ensure victory.

By the time Pilate appeared on the palace balcony, the crowd was in a frenzy. When he asked, "Whom do you want released, Jesus Barabbas, or Jesus who is called the Messiah?" the angry mob shouted, "Barabbas! Barabbas!" I was standing close enough to the balcony to see the shocked expression on Pilate's face.

Then Pilate asked, "What do you want me to do with Jesus who is called the Messiah?" The crowd shouted in a deafening roar, "Let him be crucified!"

Pilate was stunned. He calmed the crowd, which took several minutes, and asked, "Why? What evil has he done?" The crowd, now mad with bloodlust, shouted with ear-splitting volume, "LET HIM BE CRUCIFIED!"

Pilate, coward that he was, washed his hands in front of the crowd. It didn't matter. Not even Pilate would go against the will of the raving mob below. The Jesus Problem would have a satisfactory resolution.

Shortly after three o'clock, I heard the news that Jesus had died. A smile forced itself onto my lips.

The next day, my priests and I met with Governor Pilate because of a rumor we heard. One of the witnesses at Jesus' trial had testified that he heard Jesus claim he would rise from the dead after three days. I told Pilate of this and requested that he place a guard of soldiers at the tomb to make certain it would be secure. "This last deception would be worse than the first," I argued.

Pilate sat on his throne with slumping shoulders and head cradled in his hands, looking haggard and tired. He said to us, in a testy tone, "Use your own guards. I'm not wasting any more effort on this."

Though I would rather have had Pilate's soldiers at the tomb, I had to settle for his permission to station our guards there.

The next day, the first day of the week, I was going over the temple accounts with the treasurer when one of my guards burst into the room.

"Your Highness! The body of the blasphemer Jesus is gone!" he cried, with terror in his voice.

"*Fool*! What happened to the guards stationed at the tomb?" I shouted.

"They were there. But they fled from the tomb, believing that an earthquake was taking place. When they returned, the body was missing!"

I called in my chief priests, and we decided what to do. We bribed the guards at the tomb to say that while they were sleeping, Jesus' disciples had stolen the body during the night.

Lately, I have heard an incredible story of what happened to Jesus. Some of his followers are spreading an insidious lie: that he actually was raised from the dead!

Will the Jesus Problem ever go away?

Prayer

Dear Lord, help me to see Jesus not as a threat, but as a possibility for a new life. Open my eyes and ears to the truth embodied in his life, death, and resurrection. Open my heart in faith to the new life to which he calls me. In Jesus' name I pray. Amen.

Study/Discussion Questions

1. Why was Caiaphas so afraid of Jesus? What threat did Jesus pose to him?
2. Which of Jesus' teachings do you find threatening? When you are threatened, how do you react?
3. How does seeing the trial of Jesus through Caiaphas's eyes add to your understanding of it? Was it really a trial? Why or why not? What do you think Jesus meant by saying, "Destroy this temple, and in three days I will raise it up" (John 2:19)? How did his accusers use this statement against him?
4. What emotions do you imagine Jesus had during his "trial"? When have you suffered unjustly? When have you been declared guilty when you were really innocent? How is God present in innocent suffering?
5. Where are you in the story of Jesus' passion? Which character(s) do you most identify with? Caiaphas? One of the disciples? A member of the Sanhedrin? A member of the crowd that shouted, "Crucify him"? Pilate? Jesus?

Deepening Your Lenten Journey:
Suffering

- If we believe God is present in suffering, then we too should be with those who suffer. This week, focus on a person whom you know is suffering in some way (illness, family problems, financial difficulties). First, pray for that person each day. Then, explore ways you can be present with that person in his or her difficulties.
- One of the ways we suffer needlessly is to carry around a heavy burden of guilt over something we've done or haven't done. Write down things you feel guilty about and then ask for God's forgiveness for each one. If possible, make restitution for the wrongs you've done.
- Some people suffer from loneliness, especially older adults who might be alone and isolated from their families. If you are aware of such a person, pay him or her a friendly visit. You might make a greater difference in that person's life than you realize.

Sixth Week in Lent

SIMON OF CYRENE

Read Mark 15:21-41

I was overjoyed to finally see the temple dome on the horizon. The sight of the golden dome blazing in the sun always inspired me, but especially this time. Because of a storm in the southern Mediterranean, our ship had been a day late arriving in Joppa. We started the thirty-mile journey to Jerusalem last evening, just as the sun was setting. We simply *had* to be in Jerusalem before Passover, which began today at sundown.

Several of us from Cyrene made an annual pilgrimage to Jerusalem for Passover. This year, more than sixty had undertaken this arduous journey from northern Africa to our homeland. We would stay here more than fifty days, through the harvest festival of Pentecost.

As we approached the city, our camel drivers were chattering excitedly among themselves. I overheard one say, "There's going to be a crucifixion!" They directed our caravan toward the crowds that had lined the main road out of the city.

I was outraged that the Romans would carry out executions on the holiest day of the year, and I said so to my son Alexander. This was his first visit to Jerusalem. His accompanying me was a sign that he had reached manhood. (I had left my younger boy, Rufus, at home.)

As we drew near to the road on which the criminals were marching, I could hear jeers and mocks mixed with the weeping and wailing of the families of the condemned. A cloud of dust hung over the road like fog. The Roman guards were showing no sympathy, whipping and kicking prisoners who collapsed under the weight of their crossbeam. I felt sympathy for these poor, condemned wretches. Crucifixion was a cruel and slow way to die. At least *our* way of execution, stoning, was brief, even though painful.

Alexander's eyes were wide with fear and excitement as he pleaded, "Come, Father, let's go closer." I was torn over whether to let him see this march of cruelty, but now that he was a man, he needed to understand the severity of Roman justice. We edged our way through the crowd until we were at the roadside.

Simon of Cyrene   37

As we watched the procession of outlaws, we could see they had been whipped and beaten. Blood-soaked tunics were ripped where the lashes had fallen. I was about to turn away from this gory spectacle when I saw a prisoner stumbling along the road, barely able to stay upright. My eyes were drawn to his head, upon which was set a garland of thorns. Some in the crowd were mocking, "Hail, King of the Jews!" Others cried, "Rabbi, save yourself!"

Just as he drew even with me, he tripped and fell into the dirt, pinned by the weight of the crossbeam he carried. I took an involuntary step toward him, wanting to help him arise. An armored arm stopped me where I stood.

"Stand fast, Jew! Let the scum pull his own weight," the soldier said.

Another guard kicked the prisoner and said, "Wake up, Your Highness! Your royal throne awaits!" The crowd erupted in heartless laughter at the joke.

After several more vicious kicks, the soldier said, "This one isn't moving. We wouldn't want him to miss his own execution." Then he gazed directly at me. "You there! You seem like a sturdy fellow. Perhaps you'd like to be the king's cross bearer!"

I recoiled, trying to blend into the crowd. But the same armored hand that had stopped me a few moments before now grabbed my tunic. "This Jew is eager to help. Right?"

I could feel hands from the crowd push me out into the road. There was no place to hide. I wanted to run, but if I was caught I might be whipped, or worse. Also, there was Alexander to consider. What would he do if I ended up in a Roman dungeon?

So I did as I was commanded and hefted the crossbeam off the bloody shoulders of the prisoner they called "King of the Jews." The weight was not great at first, but the burden became heavier with each step I took toward Golgotha, the "skull-place," where the crucifixions would occur.

I could hear the voice of Alexander crying, "Father! Father!" as I trudged up the road. His cries were soon drowned in a sea of jeers. From these, I learned the condemned man's name: Jesus of Nazareth. It seems that he had called himself the King of the Jews and was being crucified because of this blasphemy. All the way up to Golgotha I had to listen to the insults hurled at him.

Because the crossbeam rested across both my shoulders, I couldn't turn my head to see Jesus, who was following behind me. However, I could hear the muffled thud of a Roman boot striking his back several times. The kicks were punctuated by the words, "Move it, Your Highness!"

When we arrived at Golgotha, I was relieved of my burden. The crossbeam was lashed to a pole, forming a cross. Having never been this close to a crucifixion before, I was impressed by the cold efficiency of the soldiers. After the cross was made, the prisoners were stripped of their clothes and held down on the crosses. I closed my eyes when the prisoners' hands and feet were nailed. Many of the condemned cried out in pain as they were hoisted onto their crosses. From what I had heard about crucifixion, the agony was only beginning.

I stood fixed to a spot near Jesus, not wanting to call attention to myself, but afraid to leave. The soldiers would occasionally glance at me, but they didn't dismiss me. They were busy gambling for Jesus' clothes, oblivious to the suffering around them.

I heard two criminals hanging next to Jesus mock him between gasping breaths. "Let's see you . . . destroy the temple now . . . and rebuild it in three days . . . ha!"

"Hey, King . . . why don't you . . . jump down off your cross!"

From a short distance away, some of the Pharisees and priests taunted him: "If you're the Messiah, come down from the cross, and we'll believe you." I could hear the bitter pleasure in their voices as they sneered.

I wondered what this beaten, dying man had done to inspire such hatred. Instead of returning their insults, he was silent. I looked up at his face and saw no hatred or revenge. He seemed at peace in spite of his torment.

I was shocked out of my musings by a voice saying, "You there! What do you think you're doing here?"

I stammered, "I was compelled to carry this prisoner's cross and . . ."

"So you're staying around for the fun? Get out of here, before I find an empty cross for *you*!"

Without waiting for another word, I fled Golgotha, grateful to escape. I felt guilty deserting Jesus, who would die without friends. As I ran, I saw several women in the distance who were looking in Jesus' direction and weeping. Perhaps their vigil would offer him some comfort.

When I reached the inn where we were staying, Alexander ran to meet me. He had been sobbing, thinking that I was going to be crucified with the others. I held him tightly, with the intensity of one who has cheated death. As we embraced each other, the sky became dark, and a cold wind gusted around us. This was strange, since it was only noon. The darkness lasted until three o'clock.

That night, as we gathered for Passover, my mind kept returning to the events of the day. By now Jesus would be dead and sealed in a tomb, his agony finished. A rumor had been circulating around the city that his followers said he would rise from the dead. Some said that guards had been stationed at his tomb.

As the *Shema* was recited, I stared into my wine glass and saw a face etched with anguish. At first, I thought this was my own reflection. Then I realized it was the face of Jesus! Looking more closely, I saw the face transformed by an expression of radiant joy.

Somehow, I felt certain that we hadn't heard the last of Jesus, King of the Jews.

PRAYER

Dear Lord, let me take up my own cross and follow Jesus. When I stagger under its weight, give me strength. When my steps falter, steady me. Remind me again that bearing the cross is the way to new life. In Jesus' name I pray. Amen.

STUDY/DISCUSSION QUESTIONS

1. If you had been in Simon of Cyrene's place, how would you have reacted to being compelled to carry Jesus' cross? What would have been your fears? What would you have hoped for? When have you had to carry someone else's "cross"?
2. A "cross" can be understood to mean any kind of innocent suffering. What cross have you had to bear for yourself? How did you carry this cross? Faithfully? Reluctantly? When have you been afraid to take up your own cross? What was the outcome?
3. Imagine witnessing a crucifixion. What emotions would you feel? Would the innocence or guilt of the condemned person affect your feelings? How?
4. Simon's sons, Alexander and Rufus, mentioned in Mark 15:21, have led scholars to believe that they were known to the author of Mark's Gospel and that they were Christians. What do you imagine happened to Simon after his encounter with Jesus? Is Jesus' crucifixion enough to lead one to believe in him? Why or why not?

DEEPENING YOUR LENTEN JOURNEY:
CROSS-BEARING

- On a sheet of paper, list some of the "crosses" you have carried in your life. Reflect on your list using these questions: Which crosses have been the most difficult? Which have been too heavy to carry alone? Which have led to new life?

- Help carry the "cross" of a friend or relative this week. This will mean helping to bear whatever burden (emotional, physical, financial, guilt, and so forth) this person is carrying. Remember that a shared burden is lighter.
- Make a point to read the Passion story this week (Matthew 26:14–27:66; Mark 14:1–15:47; Luke 22:14–23:56). Read with imagination, asking yourself: Where am I in the story? With whom do I most closely identify?

Holy Week

NICODEMUS

Read John 3:1-12, 7:45-52, 19:38-42

My meeting with Jesus was the most confusing and amazing encounter of my life.

My purpose in meeting him was to investigate rumors that had reached the Sanhedrin. Several members of the Sanhedrin wanted to learn more about Jesus. As members of the ruling council of seventy-one elders, we had a responsibility to discover the truth. News of the wondrous signs he had performed astounded us. Some said he had turned water into wine! One rumor in particular made me desperate to meet this man: His followers claimed he was the long-awaited Messiah!

My friends and I discussed these things secretly because others in the Sanhedrin, including Caiaphas the High Priest, had denounced Jesus as a blasphemer. They were pressuring the council to arrest Jesus and his followers. Therefore, we had to be cautious.

I arranged to meet with Jesus at night, under the cover of darkness, where there would be little chance of discovery. I went expecting to hear the teachings of a great rabbi. This encounter, however, was *nothing* like I had imagined. In the end, I left absolutely confounded.

I opened the conversation as I would with any respected rabbi— by complimenting Jesus on his reputation as a teacher sent from God. I assumed he would be flattered, since I too was a noted rabbi who taught in the temple.

Receiving no response to this compliment, I explained that only God could be the source of the signs I heard he had performed. I waited for him to reveal the purpose of the signs to me. Instead, Jesus ignored my opening speech and offered a bewildering reply.

"Very truly, I tell you, no one can see the kingdom of God without being born anew."

I prided myself on being one of the most knowledgeable rabbis in Israel, yet this response left me in the dark. I couldn't imagine what he meant by "being born anew." In typical rabbinical fashion, I asked for clarification by presenting an example.

Nicodemus   **43**

"Can one enter a second time into the mother's womb and be born?" I asked.

I knew my question was absurd, but I was seeking a way for Jesus to lead me out of my confusion. Instead, he plunged me deeper into darkness by saying that a person must be born both "of water and the Spirit."

I thought I knew what he meant by being born of water. We are all born of the water of our mother's womb. But what did he mean by a birth "of the Spirit"? Which spirit was he talking about? The Spirit of God?

Before I could ask another question, Jesus went on to say that flesh gives birth to flesh, and spirit gives birth to spirit. Again, I understood the first side of the equation but not the second. This conversation wasn't proceeding the way I had planned. My face must have shown surprise, because Jesus said, "Do not marvel that I said to you, 'You must be born anew.' "

Then he lost me completely. He spoke of the wind, how "it blows wherever it chooses, but we do not know where it comes from or where it goes." Because the word for wind also means "spirit," I was baffled. If he was saying that the spirit is like the wind, what did it have to do with this second birth? I was frustrated by Jesus' words. Why was he speaking in riddles? Why couldn't he teach plainly?

Finally, in exasperation, I blurted out, "How can this be?"

Jesus remained calm and looked upon me as a father gazing patiently upon a confused child. He asked how a teacher of my stature could fail to grasp something so simple. What he said next was painful. He said that I couldn't understand his teachings because I didn't believe in him. I felt like a son who had been chastised.

His final words were even more wounding: "If I have told you earthly things and you do not believe, how can you believe if I tell you heavenly things?"

I left knowing little more about this rabbi than when I had first walked into the room.

At a meeting of the Sanhedrin a few weeks after this, we heard a report from the temple police who had investigated Jesus. They too were astonished and confused by his teachings. They were divided over whether Jesus had claimed to be God and thus had committed blasphemy.

After hearing the report of the Sanhedrin, some members of the council wanted to arrest Jesus immediately. They argued that, even though the report was inconclusive, Jesus was a growing threat and should be eliminated.

In fear, I realized that Jesus might be arrested immediately. Though I wasn't ready to believe that he was the Messiah, neither could I condemn him. I took a risk and addressed the council.

"Does our law judge a man without first giving him a hearing and learning what he does?"

Many members were angry at my plea for a fair hearing. Some of them looked as if they were wondering whether I was one of Jesus' secret followers. But my words were enough to temporarily prevent Jesus' arrest.

Those events took place nearly one year ago. Eventually, those who plotted to arrest Jesus and have him killed were triumphant. He was crucified like a common criminal after a farce of a trial. During the trial, I remained silent. The Sanhedrin, whipped into a frenzy by Caiaphas, wanted Jesus dead. To speak in Jesus' defense would have been to risk death. Even so, I felt guilty about my silence.

You see, much had happened since my nighttime conversation with Jesus a year before. I had become a believer, although secretly, for fear that I might share his fate. My confusion had been transformed into faith. I had come to believe that this man, Jesus, was the Messiah, the Christ, the One who brought God's salvation to the world.

After Jesus' execution, Joseph, a wealthy friend of mine from Arimathea, asked Governor Pilate for the body so that we could bury our Lord. Pilate reluctantly agreed. After the body was released, I met Joseph in a garden of tombs with spices to prepare the body for burial. I brought a huge amount of aloe and myrrh; I wanted Jesus to have a burial befitting the Messiah. We anointed the body, wrapped it, and laid it in a nearby tomb owned by Joseph's family. We had to work quickly because Passover began at sundown, and no burials were allowed during this holy festival.

When I began to believe in Jesus, an astonishing thing happened. I understood what Jesus was trying to tell me on that night long ago about being born anew. The second birth has nothing to do with physical rebirth. Being born anew is to receive a new *spirit*, the spirit of Jesus. This is a spirit of love, joy, and peace. Through believing in Jesus, I was reborn into a new life. It was as if the spirit of Jesus was born within me!

A year ago, I was in the darkness of ignorance and unbelief. Now, I am in the light of understanding, because Jesus, the Light of the World, has shown me the way to a new life.

Prayer

Almighty God, who sent Jesus, the Word made flesh, lead me out of the darkness of unbelief into the light of faith. When I am confused, open my eyes to the Truth. When I fail to understand, allow your Spirit to enlighten me. In Jesus' name I pray. Amen.

Study/Discussion Questions

1. Why do you think Nicodemus was unable to understand what Jesus said about being "born anew"? When have you been confused about a teaching of Jesus? Where did your confusion lead you?
2. What led Nicodemus out of the darkness of ignorance and doubt and into the light of belief? In what ways do you identify with Nicodemus's journey of faith? What has led you to believe in Jesus?
3. Once Nicodemus believed in Jesus, what Jesus had said to him about being born anew made sense. How has believing in Jesus helped you make sense of your life? What aspects of your faith have become clearer to you? What aspects of faith are you still confused about?
4. What does it mean to be "born anew"? How would you explain this to a nonbeliever? What does it mean to be born "of water and spirit"? In what ways have you been born anew through faith in Jesus?

Deepening Your Lenten Journey: New Birth

- During Holy Week, we relive the last events of Jesus' life. The special services held during this week are of great significance to Christians. Make a commitment to attend worship services on Holy Thursday, Good Friday, and Easter. The Saturday between Good Friday and Easter could be a day of quiet reflection on the meaning of the cross and Easter.
- Although none of us remembers our "first" birth, we can imagine what it would be like. Visualize yourself coming from the dark warmth of a womb into the light and air. Imagine taking your first breath. Then draw parallels between this birth and being "born anew."

- On Easter Sunday, discover new ways to celebrate the new life that comes through the Resurrected Christ. Some possibilities: Take a walk for the sole purpose of enjoying God's creation; do a fun activity; play a special game with family or friends; deliver a lily to someone who is unable to attend Easter worship. The key is to be creative.